Basic Service Management

A 50-page introduction

to providing services

Rob England

Sensible business practices

© Two Hills Ltd 2011

Created and published by Two Hills

letterbox@twohills.co.nz

www.twohills.co.nz

PO Box 57-150, Mana

Porirua 5247

New Zealand

Published August 2011

ISBN-13: 978-0-9582969-3-9

Service Management is the potent idea that could change the way you run your organisation. This useful little book is a pocket guide on how to operate any enterprise, described from the point of view of the services it delivers. After all, delivery is what success is all about.

It describes the basics, in realistic pragmatic terms. And it is brief – we limited ourselves to 50 pages.

Whether you are in manufacturing, trades, retail, IT, public sector, not-for-profit...; whether you provide service internally to the rest of your organisation or externally to paying customers; whether you work anywhere from a small business to a government department; this book introduces you to service management.

It will get you started, get you up and running, and it will set you on the path to the advanced concepts if that is where you need to be. Or this book and its website may be all you need.

Why service management

If you are reading this book, you probably don't manage your services so much.   That gives you an opportunity to increase revenues and profitability: improving your service brings increased efficiency and effectiveness.   That means increased returns for much less investment than from improving your products or equipment.

Service management gets your whole organisation working "outside-in": talking to customers, understanding customers, thinking about yourselves in customer terms, seeing yourselves as customers see you, giving customers service that they want.

You <u>are</u> in the services business

In this century, if you run a business it is most likely a service business whether you know it or not.   Customers don't want to simply buy something any more.   They don't simply want something done.   They want to have a nice easy experience with added value – to be served.

Whether you build roads or map them, operate ports or use them, build houses or sell them, plan weddings or sing at them, care for kids or clothe them, sell PCs or scrap them, you are in a service business, even if you may not be in a "service industry".

We aren't talking about over-the-counter "may I help you?" service, the focus of a number of books.   Those books tell you how to develop the customer service interface, the experience of contact. This book is about the end-to-end process of providing services, and most of all about how to manage them.

Learning from the computer guys

This book generalises the concepts that have been recently refined in the Information Technology industry – the current "experts" in this topic (even if it doesn't feel that way sometimes).

To learn the very best way to manage services, go talk to the people in Information Technology. They have an ISO standard (20000), and lots of IT service management (ITSM) books and consultants. ITSM is the idealized best practice; the top performance goal; the world champion technique. But what they produce is typically dense and theoretical and technical. In fact almost all books on service management – IT or not - are thick, comprehensive and advanced.

The IT folk have developed Business Service Management (BSM) as an attempt to talk in terms of business services not IT services. You will find most of this BSM material has not been successfully de-geeked – it clearly shows its IT origins, and it remains inaccessible.

Sticking to the basics

Maybe you are not ready for "world champion": what if you don't even know how to hold the bat or hit the ball? And what if you don't *need* gold-standard service management, not now and maybe not ever? And what if you can't understand a word that IT people say?

Here is Basic Service Management, describing the basics you need to start in managing real business services, to get by. It will set you on the road to gold-standard service or it just may be all you need.

We have taken the central ideas from a range of sources and summarised them in plain English and pragmatic terms. Use what is good for you; get started with what we give you; then follow the references for more when you need it.

How to use this book

Read it. It is short.

Here are five tips for using this book:

1. As you read it, note ideas relevant to your organisation (there are note pages in the back of the book).

2. Go to www.basicsm.com. There you can get further help and resources, and discuss with others. You can see if we have any supplementary pages for your industry or other special interests. This book is just the right size that you can print the supplementary pages on A4 or Letter, fold them and tuck them into the book.

3. Later your organisation will need to go more deeply than this book. What areas you do that in will depend entirely on your business and your requirements. In the text we include the technical terms, buzzwords or source documents. Find the numbered references in the Resources section at the back of the book. For the other mentions, you will find some useful links on www.basicsm.com, otherwise we expect everyone to be adept at using Google.

4. When it comes time to get into service management more deeply, you need to decide at what point and in what way it is more cost effective to bring in experienced and knowledgeable people instead of inventing and learning it all for yourselves. We have made service management basic in this book but we cannot make it simple. Don't go too far without more information and help – seek professional advice before it is too late.

5. Keep it real: only improve your service management where the benefit exceeds the cost.

This is a book of four parts:

The early pages deal with more abstract concepts and business principles. If that is not your interest, hang in there – the book gets more concrete, covering operational activities and roles.

What is a service?

There are many definitions of a service: "A service is a means of delivering value to customers by facilitating outcomes customers want to achieve, but without the ownership of specific costs and risks" (ref 5). This does not help those who are trying to grasp the fundamental concept. "Economic activities that produce time, place, form, or psychological utilities" (ref 4) is only a little better. Our definition: **A service is the offering and consumption of one type of transaction.** Each transaction is not a service: the service is the provision of all the transactions of that one type to all the customers.

In the purest use of the word, services are "acts, deeds or performances: they are intangible" (ref 4). They are usually something you provide to a customer on an ongoing basis.

Products

In this book we also consider a product as a service. Products and services are really the same thing. There is a **spectrum** from product to service: every offering is somewhere between the two. Nearly every product includes a facilitating service; nearly every service includes something tangible. Much theory about "product" management, sales, lifecycles or marketing applies equally to services.

Make no mistake, in the modern world even if you sell products people **expect** a service. That is, they want you to:
- understand their needs
- help them find that they want and advise them on the best choice or at least the relevant options
- deliver it to them reliably
- make right whatever goes wrong
- then support that product for as long as they need advice, spares or maintenance

This will become even more important in this century as we move from mass manufacturing to mass **customisation** – consumers designing their own product, where every item of product is a service.

Services

If someone is getting you to provide a service - to do something for them - that is because they either **can't** or don't **want** to do it for themselves.

Either you have some capability they don't, or you can do it cheaper or better, or you are making their life easier, or there is some risk they want you to take for them. How ever they define it for themselves, they are buying **value** from you. They'll pay for it if the price is less than the value *they* perceive it to be worth.

If you are providing services to your own organisation, i.e. if your customers work for the same firm as you, then you are an "**internal service provider**" or "shared services provider". **Outsourcing** is much in vogue at the moment; getting someone external to do what you do instead.

If your customers are external to your organization, then you are in the service **industry**. Whilst selling product usually produces a single up-front payment, selling service usually gives you ongoing **revenue** for as long as you supply the service. This is a hard business model when you are starting up and need cash fast, but it is a nice model if new customers get hard to find.

What is your service?

Some house builders regard their service as sourcing materials and assembling them according to plans provided. That is not what I expect today. I am also buying their experience, their access to trusted expertise, and their advice. If I have a bad idea or choose the wrong thing I want them to tell me, and to try to convince me otherwise. If we need a plasterer, I want one they know and trust, not some guy out of the phone book - I could have done that. When things go wrong I need the builder to work out how to make it right.

I will choose based on **referral** and then on price. In turn I will refer based on **quality, cleverness, experience and helpfulness** much more than price.

So get to know your customers, and really understand what it is they are buying not what you think you are selling. Then give them what they want.

Customers

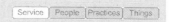

Services are **customer-focused**. Customers are never some remote external entity. They must be integrated into your service delivery, your planning and your reporting.

There is a distinction between customers and consumers. Consumers[1] **consume** your services, customers **pay** for them. They are not always the same people, depending on your industry and the services themselves.

Here is a **customer-focus maturity model**[2] to benchmark your organisation against:

> Level 1: Focus on **product.** Emphasis is on making a product good enough that buyers will seek it out. An understanding of the target market.

> Level 2: Focus on **analysing** customers, from market research and segmentation studies. Emphasis is on sales of products, and understanding customers as a market, which influences sales more than product development.

> Level 3: Focus on **understanding** customers. Emphasis on designing and/or positioning the products to solve customer problems. Your organisation changes to a more customer-centric structure and behaviours

> Level 4: Focus on meeting customer **needs**. It doesn't matter whether you produce all the inputs you provide to customers. You source all the components of a solution to help customers with their problems, either internally or from suppliers.

Have a **customer relations** function: someone who actually talks to customers before and after the sale, understands them, represents them, advocates for them, promotes and explains services, communicates your perspective, and sets expectations.

In some industries there is benefit in meeting a **council** of senior executives (preferably CEOs) of some of your major customers annually or semi-annually.

Understand

---

[1] Two industries refer to their consumers as "users": Information Technology, and the illegal drugs trade

[2] *Reorganize for Resilience*, R Gulati, Harvard Business Press 2010, ISBN-13: 978-1422117217

- your **customers**: what they like, what they need, what their problems and pains are.

- what the **market** is: where are your customers, what are they like, how are they grouped.

- how to **communicate** with them (what channels, what media), and how you can deliver to them (what channels, e.g. distributors, partners, resellers, agents).

- how to **relate** with them (e.g. sales person, account manager, onsite consultant, web subscription).

- what your **value proposi**tion is to your customers: why they should buy.

Markets

You sell services to a market. That market may be defined by **specific** customer(s) such as a parent organisation or contracted customer(s) who outsource to you. Or your market may be defined by an **opportunity**, a need that your service fulfils for multiple customers.

The **value** of your services is the value those services realise for the customers. This value usually comes from increasing, maintaining or restoring the performance of the **customers' assets**. You extract value from the customer's assets by allowing them to use those assets to achieve some outcome. The real value of your service is the value of that final **outcome** achieved by the customer. Customers will assess your services based on the value your services deliver balanced against the services' **cost and risk**.

If you repair trucks, the real value of your service is the profit from the goods moved by your customer using those trucks. If they are highly profitable trucks, then you can charge more to repair them but you had better do a good quality job that has a low risk of repeat failures or even damage to the trucks. If they are low-profit trucks moving say gravel, then you must offer low cost repairs, and customers will accept a higher risk of failure of those repairs – so long as the cost/risk is lower than your competitors.

Service management

The art of providing services to customers is called service management.

Adopting a service management approach can have a profound affect on the way your business **works** and your staff **think**. It takes us away from that introverted, bottom-up thinking that begins with what we have and what we do and eventually works its way up and out to what we deliver to the customer. Instead, with service management we change our point of view from concentrating on the internal "plumbing" of our business, moving instead to a focus on what "comes out of the pipe" – what we provide. We take an "**outside-in**" view. Starting from this external perspective we then work our way top-down into the service organisation to derive what we need and what we have to do in order to provide that service.

Service management isn't one subset of the business; it is not one activity at the end of the main supply chain. It is a different way of **seeing** the whole supply chain, the whole business that produces the services, by seeing it initially from the outside, from the customer's point of view. Therefore this book strays into general business management topics.

Seeing our business in terms of the services it provides can't help but make us better at providing them. To a customer, "better" means **more useful and more reliable,** i.e. more valuable and better quality. From the service-provider's point of view, "better" means **more effective and more efficient**, i.e. better results and cheaper.

Services have a **lifecycle**: they get proposed, approved, planned, designed, built, deployed, operated, managed, fixed and eventually upgraded, retired or suspended.

There are people who **do** that, people who **manage** that and people who **govern** it.

	Do	Manage	Govern
Plan			
Design			
Build			
Deploy			
Operate			
Fix			

Who does them in your organisation?

Most descriptions of service management are either idealised (what the perfect system looks like), or comprehensive (everything you could possibly consider), or both.

The world doesn't work like that: we don't build everything at once and we don't build perfectly first time. Don't try to do it all at once: don't try to do all areas and don't try to do all of one area.

Start

Start with the bits you **need** the most – and where the **quick wins** are - and do as much as you need to get what you need.

How to decide what you need? Don't do service management because it seems like a good idea.   Do it because there is some business improvement or result required – "a **gain** or a **pain**" - and service management just happens to be the best way to get there: e.g. lower cost customer support, fewer disastrous rollouts, happier customers, better data on products, introducing a more complex service…

So there is no substitute for looking at your own **situation** to decide what to work on.

One strategy is to properly **review** the situation. Where are you at now? Where do you need to be and by when? What is the gap? This results in a clearer big picture of where you need to improve.   Sometimes it helps to get an objective external view from experts; other times they "borrow your watch to tell you the time".

Another strategy is to simply **list** the "pains" or risks and to prioritise them, then have at them one by one. This is more of an incremental approach. The risk is that you might deal with the urgent rather than the important.

Either way, start with a business **objective**; then plan and design the solution to get it; and only then adopt the bits of service management needed in that solution.

Transform

You don't "do" or implement" or "create" service management, even though we use phrases like these all the time. You **transform** or **improve** it. Service management is there in your organisation already. Perhaps it is done badly or so little it is undetectable, but it is there. Have a mindset of building on what is already there, of improving, of increasing capability.

This brings us to an important point: **don't structure what you improve around service management theory**. For example, don't start a "Change" project to implement change control; create a "reliability" project to improve availability of services by screwing them up less often. Include some Change theory as needed. Shape the project around the outcome not the theory. Mix bits of theory where you need them to get to the outcome. To continue our example, Change is a broad topic: if you try to "do" Change you will add in work that is not directly contributing to the business outcome of reliability. It is better to take bits of Change theory and bits from other theoretical areas too and put them together into a solution for what you need right now. If services are unreliable you might also improve tracking and fixing problems, and improve availability planning, none of which are Change activities.

As another example, if customers are unhappy with the support they are getting, again you might act in several different areas:
- Tighten up response. Look for the worst metrics: maximum wait time to answer phone calls, percentage of requests resolved in first contact, average lifetime of responses...
- Improve reporting of service levels: replace perception with reality (good or bad) then show real improvement over time
- Reset expectations. Confirm agreed service levels with the customer then communicate to all consumers.

Even though this book describes the basic service management, that doesn't mean you take all of this book and adopt it right away (though it is so basic that we hope you will do most of it pretty soon).

Plan an approach to the transformation. Include steps to address **people, practices and things**, discussed in detail in the rest of this book. If the planned cost and effort is not spread near to equally across each of those three aspects that would be a cause for concern.

Improve

Modern discussion of service management often centres around service **improvement**. Most change of practices improves what is already there – we seldom are starting for scratch. You are likely doing *something*.

Improvement forever is not a given: we don't always need to get to gold-standard best practice, and sooner or later we reach a point of diminishing returns. Most of us are not at that point: we have scope for improvement and a good business case for doing so.

Even if we do get close to optimal service levels, the world changes: customer expectations, competitive landscape, the services themselves. Often the journey is not so much continual service improvement as continual service adjustment.

Sometimes a big transformational project is good to kick things off and shake them loose. On the other hand continual incremental improvement is less disruptive and unsettling than radical revolutionary change. Understand what is going to work right now for your organisation.

There are differing objectives for improvement: quality, lean/efficiency, green, customer satisfaction, revenue growth, compliance…

Create a Continual Service Improvement **programme** from the start[1]; someone owns it, it has a plan, it takes suggestions, prioritises them based on how they align with the objective(s), farms them out (small tasks or big projects), tracks them, pushes them along. **Reward** those who contribute and/or get things done. Track progress and **celebrate** success.

Don't let management design improvements alone. **Senior leaders** bring context, strategy, and customer needs. **Front line workers** bring their knowledge of how to improve operational processes and procedures. And **external consultants** bring experience, expertise, ideas from outside, and theoretical best-practice content.

Quality

A lot of improvement is about quality but not all. Cost-cutting measures might decide to reduce the quality of service in order to meet a profitability target. Better quality is **not a given**.

---

[1] On the www.basicsm.com website you can find the author's approach to developing an improvement programme, called Tipu™

There are two targets for commercial quality improvement: either closing gaps with what the customer requires and expects (**usefulness**), or fixing problems that are causing errors - defects in what is delivered or interruptions in service[1] - so as to retain customers (**reliability**).

Non-commercially-motivated service providers have a different view of quality than commercial ones. The **idealistic** service provider (e.g. artist, reformer, master craftsman) often pursues quality for its own sake not for the customer or for any goal such as profit or market share.

Quality improvement should aim at **preventing** errors not just finding them. It is better to refine procedures to reduce the number of errors produced than to inspect for them and try to fix them afterwards. So fixing problems (p43) has a lot to do with quality improvement.

Quality improvement is almost always numbers-driven. Find good **metrics** to track quality to see how you are trending. Consumers judge quality based on five factors [ref 4]: reliability (dependable and accurate); responsiveness (helpful, timely); assurance/trust/confidence (competence, believability); empathy (caring, individualised); and the tangible objects involved (presentation, appearance).

Set up a practice to define, design and verify quality: define the required results; design how to achieve them; and verify they are being achieved.

There are several formal approaches to Quality, such as Total Quality Management, Six Sigma, or Baldrige.

Quality is often standards-based, either general standards like ISO 900x or industry-specific standards.

Lean[2]

Lean is an attitude, a holistic approach, especially to developing strategy but also to planning and designing tactical systems. Lean is about accomplishing **more with less**: less physical resources (which overlaps the current trend towards everything "green"), less cost, less time, less effort. It focuses on stripping systems and processes down to only what is required to deliver what the customer wants and to maximise the delivered value.

---

[1] See the Six Sigma concepts of DMAIC and DMADV

[2] See http://www.servicemanagement101.net/files/lsm-brochure.pdf for more on Lean Service Management™

Put another way, Lean eliminates **waste**. Waste appears in the following forms: Overprocessing, Transportation, Motion, Inventory, Waiting, Defects, and Overproduction. Some speak of the "8th Waste", the waste of human potential due to poor morale, lack of training, or inefficient allocation.

Work out what parts of services actually give the customer what they want, that deliver some value. Work back from there to what resources and activities create that (the value **chain**). Optimise the bits that are part of the value chain so that service delivers maximum value. Consider removing everything else. Simple in theory.

Continue

Even though you don't have to improve for ever, **don't stop** once you have done what you set out to do, for three reasons:

1)   Anything left alone will run down. You need to keep it **alive**, keep it working.

2)   The world changes, requirements **shift**. You need to be continually adjusting.

3)   Most organisations want to continue to improve, to keep getting **better**

That is why we called it a **journey** – you are never done. Service management transformation is not a project with an end-date. Assign it to someone, make them **accountable**. It is continual not necessarily continuous: you don't have to work on it every day but you do need to keep coming back

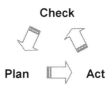

Check

Plan   **Act**

to it. Implement that formal improvement **programme**. Get into a continual **cycle** of: Check your current state; Plan where you want to be and how to get there; Act to make it happen. [1]

Too many change programmes lose momentum because management move on or lose interest. This has facetiously been described as Plan-Do-Stop. This is why you need an ongoing formal programme of work to provide continuity and permanence.

---

[1]   The most common version of this cycle is known as the Deming Cycle of Plan-Do-Check-Act, but we think Check-Plan-Act makes a more logical cycle. We first saw it in *Understanding Your Organisation as a System*, Vanguard Consulting, 2001, http://www.systemsthinking.co.uk/5-1.asp

Measuring service

External

The overall measure of service should be from a customer perspective: in terms of the business **results** delivered, not in terms of some internal performance. You need to measure enough to know if you are doing service **well** enough – usefulness and reliability - and to know if efforts at improvement had any effect.

The other power of measuring service is to give **objective** evidence to customers. Often consumers remember the bad more than the good, and the recent past more than the distant past.

Showing objective progress can help put a recent minor slip in standards into context. "Big-picture" metrics are often called key performance indicators or **KPIs**.

The classic service metric is customer **satisfaction**, measured by surveys. This can be challenging to get an accurate measure - it is subjective. It is a useful measure but not usually the best primary measure. Note that customer satisfaction is not always the same thing as consumer satisfaction: in some cases those paying for the service don't actually care how satisfied the consumers are with it. Sometimes the intent is to cut costs by having consumer satisfaction as low as possible without actually alienating anyone (e.g. after-sales support from some vendors).

The most obvious objective measure of service is its **availability**: was it available when the customer expected it to be? This seems simple enough until we define "available". If the service is too slow then it is not really available even if the "door is open".

This leads us to service **quality**, the standard of service, the quality of the customer experience. The metrics for this will differ depending on the actual service. Some minimum standard must be set, below which the service is deemed unavailable.

Once you get your operational metrics right, and understandable by customers, in some situations you can move up to reporting the *customer's* processes (and your contribution), and even move up higher again to report the **value** you provided to the customer. Put another way, report not on what *you* do but rather how you help them do what *they* do.

Internal

In addition to reporting to customers, you should track your **internal** efficiency and effectiveness for two audiences: the high level governors and the day-to-day managers. You will usually be looking to improve one or more metrics: e.g. **lower** cost, risk, cycle times, effort; **higher** quality, agility, accountability, profit.

Focusing too much on any one metric - whether you are reporting to customers, managers or governors – will lead to **distortions** of behaviour: people get driven to improve the metric even at a cost to something else. Metrics all cause this effect: the perfect metric has never been invented.

One way to reduce this problem is to use a **balanced scorecard** (or a performance pyramid, results and determinant matrix, or performance prism). The classic balanced scorecard has scores for **four** groups of metrics, typically with half-a-dozen well-chosen metrics in each group, based on the main objectives and strategies. The four groups/dimensions are: customer; financial; internal business processes; and learning and growth or innovation.

There are a number of **variations**: e.g. different dimensions specific to the business or department; nested scorecards at strategic and operational levels; or working out an overall (often weighted) score for each group and trying to improve that score. One service-oriented variant you might like to try has dimensions of effectiveness, efficiency, quality/reliability and customer value. The main point is to look at a **balance** of many metrics across different dimensions instead of making decisions based on one or two numbers.

Another good practice is to always include a **commentary** with each KPI, an "intelligence report". Numbers on their own do not tell the whole story, and behind every number is a story: why it is what it is, why it has been changing, what it is not showing…

There is a fourth audience for metrics. The actual operators also need measurement of services in order to analyse, adjust and respond: e.g. increasing requests for service require increases in capacity; a pattern of interruptions to service gives clues to an underlying problem.

People

Culture

Services are delivered by people for people to people.

There is no more important factor in service success than **people: their culture (behaviours and beliefs), their development, their motivation, and your communication.**

All change to services (new ones, improvements) is change to people: changing their attitudes, their behaviours, their daily practices and habits.

What is more, successful service providers need staff with a healthy service culture. Unlike products, services touch consumers directly. In order to deliver a service your staff must **interact** with the consumers.

It is hard to change the culture of your organisation: the beliefs and habits, "the way things are done around here". The surface effect of that culture – the "**climate**" – is easier to change: the practices and habits of people. Over time repeated behaviour and changed attitudes sink in to change the culture. So one way to gradually shift culture is to change the **rules** and procedures. If you change what people **do**, you will change how they **feel** about it and eventually what they **believe**.

As well as influencing behaviour, you can also directly influence deeper **attitudes**, and even the underlying **beliefs**, through persuasion, education and example. It takes more time and effort but it yields more results.

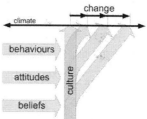

Spend a serious chunk of the money allocated for improving service on improving your people: communicate, involve, motivate, consult (pick their brains), communicate, train, incent, communicate, monitor and coach.

Technology changes at blinding speed these days but people and practices don't. Real organisational improvement must be incremental and at a human pace. Pushing change too fast breaks culture.

An important concept is "line of sight": no matter how deep they are in the "back office" functions of an organisation, try to give people line of sight to the customer. That is, keep reminding them of how they affect the customer's result and the consumer's experience. Develop **empathy** for the consumer and understanding of the consumer's **needs**. The best way to do this is to expose staff to consumers: meet and talk.

As well as bottom-up "grass roots" influences, we can also change culture from the top down, via the **leadership**: the figurehead leader, the executive team, the managers. They have a large influence on the climate or personality of the organisation and they can shift culture in only a few years by what they say and even more so by what they are seen to do. Selecting and directing them are the governors who therefore also have an influence.

Sometimes a **group** within the organisation who do not formally have a lot of power can still be influencing culture. One example is the corrosive influence of unhappy people: the most negative are also usually the most vocal. Another example is the remains of an absorbed organisation who cling on to their old culture inside the larger one (this can be good or bad but usually bad – you want everyone on the same page).

Great people make shaky practices work well, and good practices deal with poor **technology**. But it doesn't work in reverse: the best practices in the world will achieve little without getting the people right first; and without good people and good practices, any new technology is a waste of money.

Good culture is dependent on good **management**. Good culture cannot thrive in an organisation with poor management. This book is not about transforming management. There are many books on that topic[1].

Make change happen[2]

Change is driven from a high level. It needs the commitment of the top **executive**. Without that it is much more difficult.

Change is an ongoing **programme**, with no end.

Talk change over with those who will be affected by it, and those who will have to do it, and those who will have to pay for the effort.

If you have drummed up enthusiasm, get a small team together. Find one or two **champions** who will push it along. Set up a steering group of bosses and experts to keep it on track.

---

[1] We highly recommend *First Break All The Rules*, M Buckingham and C Coffman, Simon and Shuster 1999, ISBN 0-684-85286-1.

[2] This section was based on John Kotter's 8-step change model (ref 3)

Do the **vision** thing: define what you want to achieve and why, and come up with a concise way to say that. Then get the team doing some hard work selling the idea to everyone who will be affected.

Work out what might get in the way (including people), and how to overcome or remove **obstacles**.

Make people **accountable** and **measure** them. Improvement is hard unless a single person has ownership, and is answerable and empowered.

Find a few **quick wins**. Do something that shows good early results – nothing convinces sceptics better than results.

Don't invent stuff yourselves where you don't need to: draw from **outside**. This book lists some important resources: set one or two on your team to become your resident experts on service theory. Also find external people who have done what you want to do before: talk it over; hire their experience if you need to.

Use early successes to build **momentum**. Progressively work up to bigger and better things. People accept evolution more readily than revolution.

Don't lose what you achieve. Get it **embedded** in the way things are done, in people's practices and habits, in the rules and the metrics and the policy of your organisation.

We cannot stress enough that any transformation of service management - or the introduction of new services - which ignores the people aspects will at best yield less than it could have, and at worst it will fail ... sometimes spectacularly and sometimes slowly crumbling over time.

Changing people

People don't change on their own. They need motivation, communication and development.

Motivate them in these ways: by getting them involved and consulted; by showing how they benefit from the change; by making them accountable and measuring that accountability; and by incenting them.

Communicate early, communicate often, and be as transparent about decision-making as you can. Tough decisions are more palatable if people understand why. Communication is two-way: consult, solicit feedback (including anonymous), run workshops and town-halls.

Development is not just one training course. Training should be followed up, refreshed, and repeated for new entrants. Training is not enough: practical workshops, on-the-job monitoring, coaching support, local super-users and many other mechanisms all help people learn what they need to make change successful.

Employees will commit to a manager's decision – even one they disagree with – if they believe that the process the manager used to make the decision was **fair**[1]. There are three principles of fair process:

- **Engagement**. People need to feel involved and consulted in the decision-making process. They want to be heard.

- **Explanation**. People must understand why the decision was made the way it was. The decision process should be transparent.

- **Expectation** clarity. Once a decision is made, everyone should be clear on what that now means: what has changed, how things will be assessed differently. The new rules should be communicated.

Service people

Services are often **labour**-intensive industries (but technology is changing that. We now see services that are **automated**, with no human contact and few staff). There are two typical staff profiles: a small number of highly skilled staff, where you risk losing them; or larger numbers of low-skilled staff, where you must deal with churn.

Even in the most technical service industries, customer-facing skills must be a **recruiting** priority – people with a motivation to serve.

Service industries tend to have a greater **discretionary** content to the work – staff are more empowered, more autonomous than in production industries. This makes it harder to regulate, measure and assess them.

Organisation

This book does not cover the general principles of organisations and personnel but there are some important service-related points.

Consider having an **owner** accountable for

- the customer experience, the "front office", including relationship management, service levels, and support. By centralising this, they

---

[1] *Fair Process: Managing in the Knowledge Economy*, W. C. Kim and R. Mauborgne, Harvard Business Review 1997

can manage the balance between, say, impact of new services and maintaining support for the existing ones.

- each service you provide. Manage it as a product or line of business.

- each service practice (see p18). Depending on the size of your organisation, you might divide it up into Plan, Solve, Change, Provide, Assure, Respond, and Govern (as this book does), or you might break it down further into more detailed practices. The objective is to have each practice consistent across the organisation, so that it links up and flows across all organisational silos.

All these people with accountability (usually indicated by a title like Response Manager) don't have to mean more **headcount** or more work – it formalises the roles you do now. If it does increase headcount that is because you are now doing things you ought to have been doing before.

Finally, **structuring** your organisation around any body of theory such as service management is usually a bad basis. Structure around how you do business.

Suppliers

You can use third parties to provide part or all of a service, (e.g. raw materials supplier, software developer, machinery maintenance, telecoms provider, parts manufacturer, call centre, field support, debt recovery), but as far as the customer is concerned you are the **aggregator**, the provider of the service. This means you can **outsource** the execution, the management, even the audit, of some function, but you can't get out of **accountability** to your customer unless you specifically contract out, in which case they are not solely your customer any more.

So if you outsource always ensure you retain your in-house **governance** capability to direct and monitor suppliers – see Govern, p46.

Achieving the service **levels** you agree to provide to the customers is only possible if *your* service providers - the suppliers - commit to the same levels (or better) to you. For example if you commit to fix problems with the service 24x7, then you have an exposure if your supplier only supports you during office hours. You might choose to take the risk or to work around it, but you must be aware. So always compare your service providers' commitments "back-to-back" with your own commitments to your customers.

Practices

After People, the next most important consideration is Practices. Practices[1] are what the people do, the activities.

Maturity

Every organisation does nearly every practice we describe here. It is how well they do them and manage them that varies. Maturity assessments often look at how well a practice/process is **managed**, on the assumption that well-managed processes are more readily improved. Your organisation's maturity[2] for managing each practice could be:

None　　　There is no detectible trace of the practice

Ad-hoc　　Chaotic. It is done but with no consistency. How it happens depends on who does it and other circumstances

Consistent A repeatable process. It happens much the same way every time: for the same initial conditions it gives the same result.

Defined　　The practice is documented and official, and staff are trained in it – it is passed on as people come and go.

Managed　　Someone is in charge of it. We can see how well we are doing – we get metrics.

Improved　　We track how we are doing and work to make it better (up to some point of diminishing returns)

Remember, this model measures how well you **manage.** It doesn't measure how well you **perform** at delivering service, only how *equipped* you are to improve (see Improve, p8). To assess how well you actually *do* your practices, you must first have (1) a reference model of the "best practice" for your job or industry and (2) an instrument: a questionnaire or other tool for measuring consistently. For framework and methods for measuring maturity of practices, see ISO/IEC 15504 a.k.a. SPICE which has a strong IT flavour but is actually applicable to assess any set of practices.

---

[1] You will find "process" being used to mean "practice", but the term "process" is used too broadly for our tastes. We think a process is a formal thing with defined inputs and outputs. Another term you meet is "procedures" which are the practical steps to be done, including the work instructions, to perform the practice.

[2] These levels are based on the Capability Maturity Model, CMM (or CMMI). There is a CMM model specifically for service providers, see ref 2

Seven areas

There are several sources of service management theory. They all structure service management – slice it up - in different ways.

We'll divide service management practices into seven areas or domains of activity you have to do to provide services:

Plan how you will run things and what you need to do

Solve your customers' need: create a service

Evolve the way things work in your business in a controlled way

Provide the services to customers

Assure the services meet goals, requirements and regulations and are safe for you and your customers

Respond when things happen, especially when your customers ask for advice or assistance

Govern the system to ensure it meets objectives and stays within the bounds that have been set

The Plan and Assure domains are managing, Govern is ...well... governing, and the other four are doing. These are our seven names for these areas - other theoretical frameworks use different names and/or slice it differently. We have tried to keep the model generic. What we describe leads into all the other bodies of knowledge: it is compatible; it won't lead you in the wrong direction if you want to get into something deeper.

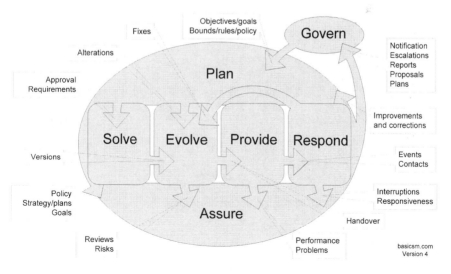

basicsm.com
Version 4

Strategic plan

At the highest level there needs to be an **organisational** strategy. That is outside the scope of this book except to say that if you need to have your own local "service strategy" (or "IT strategy" for those in that industry) then this indicates your unit is not integrated with the business. Do a local Service Strategy if you have to, but optimally there is **one** strategy for the entire organisation, which includes a service view.

If you are an internal service provider, then look at where your business is going, what the business strategy and plans are. Hopefully your department head is a part of the executive team. Write your department's role into that business strategy and plan or - if you can't do that - write a departmental plan that goes along with it.

If you do need to create a **strategic plan**, then build it up in these steps:

1) **Vision**, mission, values based on governors' directives

2) An "as-is" **assessment**, a situational analysis, a SWOT (strengths, weaknesses, opportunities, threats)

3) Strategic **goals**

4) Operational **objectives** - translations of the goals. Make them SMART: specific, measurable, attainable, relevant, time-bound

5) **Strategies**: the broad brush what you will do to get to the goals. Each strategy has one or more of the following forms, the "five Ps"[1]:
   - Plan: steer in a direction
   - Ploy: a manoeuvre – usually competitive
   - Pattern: consistent behaviour or recurring theme
   - Position: holding ground or moving into a niche
   - Perspective/personality: the way of seeing the world

6) **Tactics**: the step-by-step actions to follow the strategies

7) **Policies**: guidance and constraints

A strategy is only as good as the **communication** of it to all levels in the organisation.

---

[1]   *Five Ps for Strategy*, H Mintzberg, California Management Review, Fall 1987

Service plan

Have a **connection** with the customer. Have business relationship manager(s) who talk with key customers, and market researchers for the rest. Get **information** about what is happening, what they need. **Segment** and target your customers.

Write a **service plan**. Review it at least annually, and for any new service. A service plan might include the following plan elements:

- **Vision** and principles for SM

- **Scope** of SM

- **Objectives** to be achieved by SM

- Context and alignment with **business** strategy and plans

- Service **strategy**
  (market, offerings, service models, service portfolio and demand)

- Service **policy**
  (decisions, directives, priorities, constraints)

- **Roles** and responsibilities for SM
  (planning, implementation and execution)

- **Transformation** of SM
  (current state, desired improvements, approach to change)

- Responding to **external** events
  (legislation, regulation, mergers and acquisitions, changing business requirements...)

- **Practices** to be executed

- **Interfaces** and coordination between practices
  (collaboration between teams, OLAs, supplier interactions)

- Interfacing with **project** management
  (operational readiness: non-functional requirements, project liaison, operational acceptance testing)

- **Resources**, facilities and budget

- **Governance** of SM
  (strategy, risk, delegation, performance, compliance, culture, capability, procurement)

- **Tools** to support the practices

- **Quality** management, audit and CSI

When planning your services, your plan should consider what **new** services customers are going to get in the future. Is the business rolling out a new product? Are there plans to branch out into new lines of business, or to merge or acquire?

For each proposed **new** service:

- **forecast** demand.

- agree with the customers or decide for yourself (depending on your situation) what **service levels** they get: hours of operation, availability (percentage they can expect it to be working), responsiveness of support (how high to jump).

  You might offer a few alternative levels of service (e.g. gold, silver). If you don't set level targets for each service, then have generic service level targets that apply to groups or types of services. Note: service levels are often treated as a goal to shoot for. They are better considered as a minimum acceptable limit.

- determine what **requests** consumers can make: new/change/delete, access, copies of documents, bookings etc This is a great way of defining and understanding the service.

- determine what will be the **impact** on the organisation's ability to deliver other services. Plan for more capacity (people, equipment, power, IT resources...). Plan for more tools to manage it. Most of all plan for more people to operate it. Ask for the money – make sure it is in the budget.

- plan for the worst. Think about **disaster recovery** (see Assure, p38). Think of scenarios where your systems can't be fixed; they have to be rebuilt or run somewhere else. How?

For each **existing** service:

- **forecast** demand.

- review **trends** with customers and the service owner.

- determine required **improvements**.

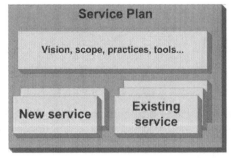

Service portfolio

The service portfolio manages all services across their service **lifecycle**: requested, planned, in development, live and retired.

Your **catalogue** of services (see Provide, p34**Error! Bookmark not defined.**) is a subset of the service portfolio. The catalogue describes only the live services.

Plan your services as a **portfolio**, not individually. Decide new services and changes to services (as proposed in the Service Plan) based on

* **organisational** strategy and policy

* where it fits in the service **portfolio**

* available **resources**

* your organisation's ability to **deliver** both the project and ongoing operation

Change Portfolio

There are many aspects to change but we will consider three levels:

* **Organisational change**: transformations to the way you do business.

* **Solution change (service portfolio)**: new services / products.

* **Operational change management (change control)**: adjustments, fixes, updates, upgrades, moves/adds/changes.

These are not crisply distinct; they blur into each other, which is why you should consider managing them all as one change **portfolio** for your organisation. The **smaller** the organisation, the less point there is in distinguishing between different areas of change. Within the portfolio, groups of changes can be managed as a **programme** of work. And each significant change should be a **project** (see p30).

There is benefit in managing all changes **holistically**, in a portfolio(s). There is never enough **money** or **resources** for all the changes you need to do. Everything seems to be important. But if you try to do them all you will use up all the funds, exhaust the company, and break "business-as-usual' operations. So someone has to make the hard calls about what gets priority now, what gets pruned but goes ahead, and what just has to wait.

A portfolio is all about **balance**, some would say juggling. Demand for changes must balance **strategic** requirements (e.g. as dictated by service portfolio) and the potential **value** of those changes against available

resources, the **impact** on existing services (Operations), and the finite **rate** at which the organisation can grow.

Change portfolio is an **investment** portfolio. You must evaluate, prioritise, and **select, defer or reject** new investments in the context of managing and **optimising** the overall portfolio of existing investments. Then you **manage and monitor** that portfolio of investments through their lifecycle to ensure you are still getting the expected value.

The bigger the picture when you do that, the better. If you are making decisions across only new products/services or accounting for only the impact on the operations team, then you will create distortions or negative impacts elsewhere, and resource won't get allocated optimally for the whole organisation. Make big-picture portfolio calls: e.g. this operational change can go ahead even though it means this new product needs to be delayed.

Your organisation's projects (and programmes of work) may already be managed as a *project* portfolio. This is not the same thing as a *service* portfolio: **projects** only deal with *changes* to the services, not the stable operating services (the catalogue). And project portfolio is not the same thing as a *change* portfolio: there are changes bigger and smaller than projects.

A portfolio of organisational, service and operational changes is the most **comprehensive** mechanism for making business decisions about priorities, spending, and resourcing as it considers current operations as well as proposed changes. It takes into account the requirements of service portfolio, but also accounts for even larger organisational transformations (e.g. a merger or re-branding). It includes projects under way and projects pending. And it takes into account the operational changes managed by change control. We allocate funds and resources holistically across this whole portfolio, balancing the competing priorities.

This is the **author's** model of interlocking portfolios. There are many differing models of change and how it interacts with services and projects, and not one generally accepted view. N.B. There is a school of thought that all management can be understood in terms of portfolios[1]: services, projects, changes, assets and so on.

Business case

All change should have a justification that is understandable at an enterprise level – a business case.

A business case claims certain **benefits** can be obtained from **outcomes** or outputs of a **solution** delivered by the **proposal**. The business case explores whether a change (usually a project)

is...	for the...	within the...	meaning...
desirable	enterprise	portfolio	we are prepared to pay that much for the expected benefits
achievable	owner	programme	the *benefits* can realistically be achieved by this proposal
viable	solver	project	the proposed solution can be delivered as specified

(The "solver" is whoever is responsible for building, acquiring, or otherwise supplying the solution created by the project to deliver the defined outcomes which will produce the expected benefits).

All business cases should gather lessons learned from the past.

Unlike common practice, a business case should be examined not just before approving the change, but throughout performing the change. If the business case ceases to stack up on all three criteria – desirable, achievable and viable[2] – then the change should be halted. The business case should also be reviewed at intervals after the change is completed to ensure that the claimed benefits are being obtained.

---

[1] E.g. *Taming Change with Portfolio Management*, P. Durbin and T. Doerscher, Greenleaf 2010

[2] This principle come from the PRINCE2™, a detailed project management methodology produced by the British government and widely adopted worldwide http://www.ogc.gov.uk/methods_prince_2.asp. PRINCE2® is a Registered Trade Mark of the Office of Government Commerce in the United Kingdom and other countries.

A customer wants a new type of service or your organisation wants to launch a new product/service. Once approved, create a **solution** to give it to them. In the Solve domain, we are not building one order for a consumer, we are building the production line, the delivery mechanism, to provide multiple service transactions to consumers – we are setting up the infrastructure to provide services to customers. We are creating the massage table not the massages.

Design a service[1]

1) Identify the target <u>market</u>

Look at the overall market, the competitive environment, and your internal capabilities; then decide on the target market, i.e. the groups of customers you wish to serve. Identify their **needs** and target one or more of them for your solution.

2) Develop the service <u>concept</u>

Describe what elements make up the service and what results they deliver. Understand the value of the service to the customers in the target groups, how it meets their needs, what constitutes "good". Decide how the service is to be positioned, the desired perception, any differentiators. Generally you can compete by[2] (a) being narrowly focused (location, group of customers, other niche), (b) by having a differentiator, or (c) on price.

3) Plan the <u>operations</u> of the service

Create **plans and policies** for all the operational aspects of the new service: service process, customer experience, daily operations (including support response), infrastructure, facilities, finance, marketing, HR, and management control of quality and costs. Develop an **operating model** of who will provide all these capabilities: your own staff, service providers,

---

[1] For more on this topic, see *Managing the Service Economy*, J Heskett, Harvard Business School Press, Boston 1986. Also see *Service Management and Operations*, ref 4,.

[2] *Competitive Advantage: Creating and Sustaining Superior Performance*, M Porter, The Free Press, New York 1985,

suppliers, vendors, even customers and consumers themselves. You need to maximise the ratio of value (determined as part of the concept) to cost of operations. If you want the service to be high value, you need high quality. If it will be perceived as low value, you need to drive costs down. Cost of delivering a service is harder to work out than the value derived from it. To assign costs to services you may need some crude rules-of-thumb – it takes some advanced processes to do it accurately[1] so don't get too hung up on it.

4) Design a service delivery system

Determine the **features** and **capacity** of the system so as to be able to deliver customer value, with both the required cost and quality of operations:

- people all trained and enthused
- roles and jobs defined
- facilities, infrastructure and technology (machines, software, vehicles, buildings, plant), their layout, and staff to manage and operate and maintain it
- a value chain (or network): suppliers, resellers and other partners collaborating to produce…
- a transaction engine, the system that delivers the day-to-day service
- a deliverable coming out the end
- metrics and target-levels: what is "enough" and what is "good"
- and processes and work procedures to make it all work. Map and optimise service encounters. Build in data collection.

Design for the customer **experience** e.g. minimise waiting, multiple encounters, passing from person to person.

Also design for your actual service providers. Design the back office to support the front office; empower front office **staff**; introduce tools for efficiency and effectiveness.

In many industries, selection of **location** and **site** will make or break a service, as will the **layout** of the facilities. Don't underestimate the importance of physical design.

From the early design stages make sure you plan for putting the solution into **production**. Make it work to the levels promised to customers.

---

[1] For example Activity-Based Costing (ABC), but this has fallen out of favour due the cost and complexity of implementing it. The latest trend is "lean accounting".

Provide facilities for those supporting it to diagnose and correct. Create support procedures and train operational staff. Plan for availability (p35) and continuity (p36).

5) **Plan** the implementation

Have a formal project **plan** for the rollout. About a **third** of the effort should go on **people**-oriented activities, one third on **practices**, and one third on technology/facilities/**things**. It is OK to diverge from that, but it is also OK to ask why.

Make sure the operational **budget** for current and future years includes the (increased) cost of **operating** and **supporting** the new service.

Supply and demand

Understand how you are going to **balance** supply and demand. Services are **perishable** – they cannot be stockpiled for later consumption.

Design as much **flexibility** of **supply** as you can:

- overtime
- floating staff, part-timers, temps
- cross training so staff can shift roles
- outsourcing
- rental equipment and facilities
- customer contribution to their own services
- automation

Demand is driven by a range of factors:

- pricing, and pricing structures (e.g. Yield Management)
- scheduling (appointments, available hours)
- education of customers
- complementary services
- advertising and marketing promotion
- queuing and gating

Find ways to **predict** demand, to **spread** or **delay** demand (e.g. discounts for off-peak), and even to **reduce** demand when necessary (e.g. increase pricing, stop advertising) to avoid customer disappointment.

Managing solutions

Have some rules around service design: an **architecture** of how you want all your solutions to hang together, so you can have preferred

specifications. If a new solution doesn't fit those preferred specifications then you will need to budget **extra** money for operating and supporting it.

Almost all services these days involve a **value chain** (or network) of multiple service providers joining up to deliver the final service. Manage all your **suppliers** to make sure their service commitments to you line up "back to back" with your commitments to customers – see Suppliers, p17.

Manage new solutions as part of **Change** (next page). Manage each new service (all of the five steps above) as a formal **project**.

Have a formal **handover** of a solution to production operations. Those taking responsibility for it have a right to assess it before accepting it. Those creating it should help run and support it for a **warranty period**. Before the project is disbanded and the service builders all run off, ensure enough information is **documented** and shared to be able to support, fix and change it.

Equally important, ensure enough **knowledge** of the system has passed to the team of those who will have to support, fix and change it. The best way to do this is to have operational people work on the design and build of the service (or builders who go on to work in operations). Training at handover is a poor substitute.

Checklists

One simple yet **important** mechanism produces proven results in consistency and improvement when adopted: checklists[1]. The use of checklists during procedures will **reduce** error levels and **improve** performance. There isn't room in a 50 page book to include checklists but you can find free up-to-date service management checklists (and contribute more) at www.basicsm.com. Here is a sample:

Objective: to ensure everything is as it should be before approving a change request. This is a Do-Confirm checklist: run through this just before approving a change.

- ☐ Is the change correctly categorised e.g. as Normal, Major, Emergency or Standard?
- ☐ Is the right person authorising the change?
- ☐ Is the change record linked to the affected asset(s)
- ☐ ...and the affected service(s)
- ☐ has the service impact been assessed?
- ☐ Has the Change Advisory Board (if applicable) reviewed and approved the change?
- ☐ Is a procedure of steps clearly defined and tested?
- ☐ Is the change scheduled and can it be done in the alloted time?

[1] *The Checklist Manifesto*, Atul Gawande, Metropolitan Books 2009, ISBN 978-0805091748

All changes should be managed together as a **portfolio**, as part of Planning (see p23). At some point, all changes - large or small, organisational or operational - **move** from Solve (designing and building them) into a "live" state (see Production, below). That movement of changes needs to be **controlled** to minimise risk and protect operations – that is what Evolve deals with – managing the change to the operational environment.

Project management[1]

Manage changes. That sounds obvious but many organisations baulk at spending the money for change and project managers. Managing a change takes time and skills, but the investment of that extra 10% pays off in more changes being **successful** and on **time** and on **budget**.

For any change above quite a small threshold, make it into a formal **project**: plan and control it. Base the threshold on **risk** and potential **impact**, not just size.

On any but the smallest projects, a good professional project manager repays their fees in costs, risks and over-runs controlled on the project.

Every project should have a governing body – a project board - which represents the enterprise, solver and owner interests, with a single decision-making executive in charge. The manager running the project should be separate from the board and report to them.

Manage a large or risky project in stages, in which you re-assess the justification and the plan at the end of every stage: do you proceed? what should you adjust? At the start of each stage, the board commits the next portion of resources (funds, people...), and the project manager plans how to use them to deliver the outcomes of that stage.

Every project should include assurance: either the board or people they appoint should both challenge and advise those working on the project to assure that policies, rules, plans, specifications and standards are being followed.

---

[1] Some of these principles of project management come from PRINCE2™

Every project should set up what comers after it: ongoing ownership, operation and maintenance of what was built; ongoing improvement; ensuring the benefits are realised; and measuring the actual results over time.

Production

Put a "fence" around everything that provides services to consumers; i.e. define a **boundary** and call it your Production area. **Restrict** who can change Production. This includes facilities, equipment, stock, software, documentation and spares.

Get some **control** over **all** the changes to Production. Define what is considered **administration** and therefore not covered by change-control. Administration activities should still be access-controlled and audit-trailed.

Change control

To start with, make sure all changes get **recorded** somewhere central.

Later, make sure they are recorded **beforehand** and that the **schedule** is planned. Is this a good time? What else is going on? Can we batch these changes up and do them together? Can we have a regular time we do this stuff? **Publish** the upcoming schedule regularly: usually weekly, sometimes real-time.

Once you plan your changes in advance, set up a way to **approve** all changes. There is a set of approvals required, depending on the size and complexity of the organisation:

- Business owner of the change
- Operations
- Change coordinator

In addition to the approvals, many organisations will want to set up a group of **stakeholders** to **review** changes, an "advisory board", to make sure all implications have been considered. Make a list of the people they should **consult** depending on the impact of the change.

Don't approve a change unless you understand the **risks** and the operators know how they are going to **back** the change out or **restore** things if it goes wrong. Do some **policing** to make sure folk aren't sneaking changes in.

Once changes are approved and nobody is subverting the controls, define (carefully) what types of operational changes are "**standard**": they *don't* need approval *because they are low risk* (not all easy or small changes are low risk and not all low risk changes are small or easy). They still need to be written down and often need to be scheduled too.

Require that a change is **ready** before it gets the OK to go into production.

- Has it been **tested**?
- If it is a new system/product, have we worked out how to **support** it? Trained the staff, procedures to operate it, procedures to fix it, vendor support contract?
- Have we got enough **information** about it? Manuals, documentation, vendor details?

Environment

Which brings us to the next point: know **what** you are changing. A good start is to know about all the things in your **environment**. Some of these are **assets**, which crudely are the things that come through procurement – so that is a good source to start with in listing all the things in the production environment.

Some things are not assets in the sense of what you buy (and depreciate), such as documents, people and places. Other things are conceptual or virtual, such as systems or the services themselves.

One way to record things is to **capture** them as they come into production, like the procurement example, or like all the information about the things in a project that gets rolled out. In theory, if you do Change properly you will know about them all. But in reality this is usually a "leaky" approach: things get into production **undetected** – e.g. IT devices like laptops and wireless modems. So at intervals you also need to **discover** or audit or stock-take what is in production to check against what you think is there.

For more on "things" see Tools/technology/things, p44.

Agile

Agility is about rapid iterative development of ideas (e.g. in Information Technology, or business processes). Some of the key ideas about being agile are:

- Break the task up into many smaller quick **iterations**
- Work closely with the business **owner** who wants it, and if possible with **customers and consumers**
- A **team** does everything required to produce a **finished** system on every iteration, to get the system "live" to try it, and maybe to stop there once the result is satisfactory
- Face-to-face **discussion** is preferred to written communications
- Make each iteration **time-bound** not scope-bound: if you aren't going to make the deadline, don't move it - cut what you are trying to achieve.

Review

Follow up on changes. Did they **work**? Did we get the **results** we expected? What can be **learned** for next time? Did they get all **approvals** they needed? A **successful** change is one that achieved what it said it would, not a change that didn't break anything.

Dissect changes that **fail**. Try to identify the **causes** of failure and **prevent** a recurrence. Most accidents have multiple causes acting in conjunction, so look for more than one.

Formal projects should get additional follow-up some time after completion to ensure they delivered the **return** they said they would in the business case for doing the project. If projects didn't deliver as expected, then look at how business cases are written; how the decisions are made (see Portfolio, p23); how projects are managed; and how the value is measured.

Marketing

Service marketing is different from product marketing: e.g. product marketing often associates products with intangible concepts such as **emotions**, whilst service marketing links services to tangible concepts to make them more **real**.

In general we are not selling ownership of a service, just the **right** to **consume** transaction(s). In addition to the four elements of the traditional product marketing mix – **product, price, place and promotion** – we must also deal with **process, physical evidence, and participants** - the interaction of customers and staff (ref4).

In services, the linkage between customer **loyalty** and profit is strong, and the cost of **acquiring** new customers is generally high.   So service marketing is as important after the sale as before.

Catalogue

Have a catalogue of services. It is good to have two views of this: one a **brochure** written in customer's terms, and one an **internal** document describing how you provide those services.

If you have more than a few dozen services on the list, think about ways to group them. Nobody will read it if there are too many.

As each customer signs up to take a service, have an **agreement** describing the service **levels** to be achieved, terms and conditions, and arrangements for **support, payments** and so on. There are two main service level target metrics: **availability** (see p39) and **responsiveness** of support (see p44). You will most likely want a standard template for these service level agreements (SLAs), with generic default targets. Rather than defining rules and obligations for a customer, consider framing them as customer **rights and responsibilities**. This has the same effect with a more positive tone.

In the internal view of the catalogue, document where to find all the **information** about each service, and what things the service **depends** on, usually systems such as warehousing, and assets such as plant or computing (see service plan, p21).

A possible third view of the catalogue presents the "menu" of **requests** consumers can make for each service. There can be other views too for different audiences, e.g. finance.

Operations

Marketing functions that would be separate in a product business are more part of mainstream operations in a services organisation, such as customer **satisfaction** monitoring, customer **retention** and consumer **behaviour** analysis. The line between marketing and operations blurs and the two teams must work more closely.

Likewise the traditional separation of product production from the front-office customer-facing functions disappears in a pure service organisation: a service is "produced" during the interaction between front-office staff and the customer. Operations is not a back-office function. The service is presented to consumers by Operations at service **touch points**. That **service encounter** makes or breaks the customer experience. The failings of an individual server will be seen by consumers as reflecting on the whole organisation.

It is important to have some way to manage service **demand** otherwise service levels may fall too low if Operations are overloaded. If services are not charged based on the amount consumed (see **Error! Reference source not found., p**Error! Bookmark not defined.**)** then some other mechanism is required: limited access, rationing, caps.

In addition to the capabilities to directly deliver a service, there are additional capabilities needed to manage the supporting functions and resources: finance, procurement, stock control, distribution, facilities, security, maintenance, HR…

Customer **support** (see Respond, p42) blurs with the operational function as well. Service-providing staff should be able to respond to consumer requests and issues, or at least be able to log them and summon help.

Support

An integral part of supplying a service is providing help and support for that service. The support **model** must be designed as part of the service. Support is provided at four levels:

Level 0 support is when consumers resolve their own requests. Put as much help/support **information** as you can into the **public** domain – it saves support effort and doubles as a marketing tool.

Level 1 support is provided by a service desk, the trendy name for a helpdesk. Provide a **single point of contact** for all consumer requests. Although it is a single point, the service desk can and should have multiple **channels** to get to it, e.g. over the counter, phone, email, webpage. In the modern world, other channels involve seeking out consumers in the **virtual** world: forums, conversations, streams. You  need to pick up on problems, check the accuracy of advice being passed around, and offer help of your own. For more on the activities of a service desk (see Respond, p42).

Level 2 is the people who have the knowledge to **resolve** requests – the service desk will refer anything they can't solve themselves to the Level 2 teams. These could be dedicated response teams or specialist people in other roles.

Level 3 have the advanced skills to make changes to **fix** problems.

Funding

Consumers consume; customers pay. There is always some mechanism to get **paid** for service, e.g. a fixed annual budget for an internal service provider, or a credit card payment over a counter.

If funding is **fixed**, not related to the amount of service consumed, as may happen with internal service providers, then there is the risk it will become an all-you-can-eat buffet with consequent wastage. You can cap usage ("one plate per customer") but this places limits on those who genuinely need more, annoying consumers and costing you revenue.

If funding is based on the level of **consumption**, as usually happens when you sell a service, then you have more hope of managing **demand**: you bill for what is used (it is "a la carte not a buffet"). This requires a **pricing** mechanism for each service (and usually each level of service) as well as the ability to **track** and record the transactions (who used what) in a way that is reliable and clear and not easily repudiated (denied). Sometimes the complexity of setting this up and operating it outweighs the benefits. In other businesses it is fundamental.

Retiring services

As part of managing the portfolio of services, always look at the possibility of retiring services when they no longer provide enough **value** to customers or **profit** to your organisation, or if they present too much **risk**. The primary considerations are **communication** (make sure there are no surprises about it happening or the timeline) and **transition** (determine the path out for everyone and all facilities, equipment, systems and resources.). The actual decommissioning and shutdown are the final step.

Assure

"Assure" is a general term we use here for making sure, making safe. Make sure of performance, compliance, availability, security, and risk. Assurance should challenge and support those they assure.

The assurance owner reports back to managers for the daily **operation** of the organisation and reports to governors for the monitoring of **directives**. Regularly check customer satisfaction, customer needs, internal profitability, compliance and service levels delivered. The results are used in planning **improvements** and **corrections**. Set **thresholds** and if the results go outside those bounds, then treat it as an incident to be handled (p42). Check **suppliers** at least as closely as your own organisation.

Risk[1]

For many organisations, risk is the governors' primary monitoring concern, closely followed by performance. Risk activity should be embedded in every function of the organisation: (operations, solutions, facilities, service, marketing, HR, finance...). They should all **identify** risks, **track** them and attempt to **mitigate** them.

There should be a **centralised** risk function as well: a single accountable person maintaining a central risk **register**, investigating and **assessing** the reported risks, and **summarising** risk for management and governance.

Risk can be thought of as a way of looking at everything the organisation does, just as Service is also a perspective on everything. It is good to own and control both Risk and Service centrally, but they are part of everything the organisation does and everybody shares some responsibility. You need to **train** and **remind** people.

Security, Problem, Compliance and Availability practices can all be thought of as specialised kinds of risk, as subsets of risk management.

Performance

Measure your **customer performance** (service levels for availability and responsiveness; value of the service to the customer) and check them against the agreed levels.

---

[1] See the standard ISO 31000:2009 for principles and generic guidelines on risk management

Report regularly to customers so they know what a great job you are doing, or at least that you are improving.

The level of **quality** (usefulness and reliability) you need to deliver depends very much on your business and what the customers demand. Do quality assurance checking and reporting if you need to. Measuring the quality of products is easier than of activities.

Measure your **internal performance** (efficiency and effectiveness): profitability, turnover, efficiency. Look at your existing reporting: does it allow you to break it down by service to see the value of each service to you?

Some of the **challenges** in measuring services are:
- defining the scope of a service – what is and isn't part of it
- the need for slack capacity (see Supply and demand, p28)
- improvements tend to be more gradual than in production industries
- it can be hard to find clear metrics or to define what constitutes good performance.

Availability

A service is available if a consumer can get **access** to it and execute a transaction within **agreed** service levels. It should be counted as not available if it is too slow, too poor, or not there at all.

Measuring what availability you are achieving is an important part of performance for many types of service (not all: focus on it only if customers care).

Of equal or greater importance is proactively **planning** to be able to deliver availability in the **future** in response to changing conditions: growth, new services, new technology, mergers and acquisitions, cutbacks and layoffs.

So make an Availability **Plan**, have someone own it, and review it a few times a year. **Inputs** are business plans and trends, internal trends (e.g. capacity), and performance results. **Outputs** are a new plan, and requirements for the rest of the team to meet it: more people, more equipment, more capacity, new systems, better process…

Capacity

In order to support availability planning, it is important to **track** capacity of all resources: people, funds, raw materials, stock, plant, facilities, IT (network, storage, servers…). Track how much reserve there is, and how much is being used. Report the **trends** to availability planning.

Forecast how much capacity will be needed based on the predictions of the availability plan, and report that back too.

Continuity

Another aspect of availability is **preparing** for major events that overload the day-to-day ability to restore service, i.e. "disasters".

In some organisations, the cost of disaster **contingency** is too high. But at the very least think about it, realise this, document the known risk, and **insure** against it.

In most organisations, disasters can be **survivable** if prepared for. Spend a day with a core team dreaming up disaster **scenarios** (natural, economic, industry-specific, social…) and the **response** to them. **Rank** them by a combination of both impact and likelihood. Then come up with the smallest set of **responses** that will cover the top scenarios.

Make sure responses deal with the possibility of decision-makers and key operators being **unavailable** (disabled, unable to get to work, or out of communication).

Don't stop there. A plan is only a plan. **Implement** the contingency preparations – every day without them is a day at risk of wiping out the organisation. **Test** them, at least annually. **Rehearse** the scenarios.

The last step is to create a **mitigation** program to try to prevent disasters rather than react to them, e.g. move facilities away from a flood-prone area; install better fire-control system etc

Compliance

Know what other **standards** you have to meet besides the agreed service levels, such as contractual, legal, industry and regulatory requirements: safety, privacy, quality, fitness, fiscal, personnel…

Also track compliance with **internal** policies, bounds and rules.

Have somebody **own** compliance. **Communicate** compliance requirements to the affected people (staff, partners, suppliers, even consumers). **Audit** and report on compliance. Treat any non-compliance as a risk (see p38).

Security

The aspects of security most relevant to services are **information** security and **physical** security. The basics of information security are[1]:

- Protect information/systems/networks from damage by viruses, spyware, and other malicious code.
- Provide security for your Internet connection.
- Install and activate software firewalls on all your business systems.
- Patch your operating systems and applications.
- Make backup copies of important business data/information.
- Control physical access to your facilities, especially to the computers and network components.
- Secure your wireless access points and networks.
- Train your employees in basic security principles.
- Require individual consumer accounts for each employee on business computers and for business applications.
- Limit employee access to data and information, and limit authority to install software.

The basics of physical security are:

- Ensure the safety of employees and everybody who comes onto your premises
  - o Safety planning and communications
  - o Management of hazardous materials
  - o Access control and tracking
  - o Freedom of movement and exit
  - o Threat monitoring, detection, response (fire, bomb, intruder, disaster)
- Protect the integrity of your systems
  - o Access prevention harder than any expected intrusion
  - o Zoned access – high security inner zones surrounded by lower security operational zones and low security public zones
  - o Authorised entry to zones with authentication suitable to the security level
  - o Restrict resources to within the appropriate zone
  - o Audit trail of entry and exit
  - o Access control and tracking of mobile resources
  - o Reliability of supporting utility systems: power, water, cooling, telecoms, internet. Introduce backup and/or redundancy as necessary.

---

[1] NIST Small Business Information Security: The Fundamentals http://csrc.nist.gov/publications/drafts/ir-7621/draft-nistir-7621.pdf

Recall that it is cheaper to keep a customer than to find a new one. Good response to consumer requests is simple good business.

Supposedly[1] you will have happier customers if things go wrong but you fix them well than if things never went wrong at all.

Record

Record all **interactions** with your consumers, whether by phone, email, Twitter or accosted in the hallway. It is important to people that you remember last time they contacted you.

Provide a **single point of contact** with multiple channels to access it (see Support, p 35). Discourage consumers from contacting **specific** people. Steer them towards the service desk and reward them for using it by giving them good enough service that they will use it again. Recognise support **work** only if recorded by the service desk: that will incent staff to steer consumers there.

Keep a **record** of everything you need to respond to. Mostly you need to respond to a request or issue or complaint or booking or order or other requirement from a consumer.

Track all your responses and record what you did about them and close them off (**tell** the consumer!). If you can, have a way to link interactions to the related response. Remember they may call several times about the same thing.

Incidents

If a consumer doesn't get service at the **expected** level, service management calls it an "incident". Not every incident involves a consumer though: you can respond to an **internal event** such as a warning message on some piece of equipment or a stock below a threshold level that tells you a service is degraded or in danger of being affected.

An incident is just one type of response and should be tracked and handled along with all other responses, *but with high priority, and with*

---

[1] We heard it at a conference. We have been unable to find the reference.

a focus on restoring the service. Focus on getting the service back to the consumer by either **fixing** the fault or finding a **workaround** to get them working.

Have criteria to decide if it is a **major** incident. In that case, have a special process to **mobilise** staff and suppliers, **escalate** to senior managers and customers, perform emergency **communications**, **manage** the response closely, and decide if you need to go to a disaster-level (continuity) response.

Problem

Something else you need to respond to is a problem. Didn't we just do that? No. If ten consumers tell us they have an incident, there might be one underlying **cause**: that is the problem.

With an incident, our focus should be on restoring the service to the consumer, and often there is some workaround we can do to get them back up and running but that doesn't necessarily fix the problem which affected them in the first place. If an alligator bites someone, you fix the incident with bandages and maybe surgery. To fix the problem you shoot the alligator before it bites again. Staff should create problem records whenever

- incident response identifies a cause but can't immediately fix it
- incident responders don't know what the cause was
- something is clearly broken
- there is a suspicion something is wrong

Track all your problems (prioritise, work on them, follow up the slow ones), and **record** what you did about them, and close them off as you fix them or decide to live with them (if they are too hard or expensive to fix).

It is not the bosses' job to solve problems. Problems don't get escalated. The old manager's mantra is "Bring me options not problems". Those doing operations know best how to fix them.

In order to fix a problem (or an incident) you quite often have to do **root cause analysis**. There are techniques you can use to do this[1]. Some argue that there is no **single** root cause of problems. It generally takes several causes together to create a problem – they have to "line up" in some way. The first and most obvious cause you find is seldom the end of the story: keep asking "**why**" until the answers are not useful. Finding root cause is

---

[1] e.g. Kepner-Tregoe analysis or Ishikawa diagrams

not necessarily about assigning **blame** – it is about removing cause. Complex systems are in fact permanently broken, so when they actually fail it may be nobody's fault.[1]   On the other hand there could be **negligence**.

Once you are tracking and dealing with problems, the next level of maturity is to "kill the alligators before they bite you": **proactively** seek out problems and fix them.   When you are really good you will forestall them and prevent them ever existing.

This register of problems is closely linked to your register of **risks** and you may want to record them in one place.   An unfixed problem is one kind of risk: a risk that it will cause more interruptions to service.

Interruption

Which brings us to the last thing to keep a record of: interruptions to service, i.e. the actual period of the outage.   There might have been many incidents because lots of consumers called up, but only a few interruptions to the service before the problem was solved.   If you keep track of those interruptions and their duration, you have the facts when talking to the customer about how good the service availability has or hasn't been.

Report

All those records stop you dropping the ball.   They help keep you organised and prioritised.   But the other big payoff is **analysing** the data to look for trends.   What brand of equipment has the most problems, which consumers complain the most, which services have been flakiest: there is great value there to help you improve your service.

Responding

Once you have records of the tickets you are dealing with (responses, problems, interruptions), start getting smart about how you handle them:

- Make sure someone **owns** every ticket, and only one person, and you can tell who that is.

---

[1] *How Complex Systems Fail*, Richard I. Cook, MD
http://www.ctlab.org/documents/How%20Complex%20Systems%20Fail.pdf

- **Match** tickets to other tickets to see what works, and to recognise patterns

- Build up recorded **information** on the services and systems. Give responding staff access to information and training, kept in a knowledgebase.[1]

- Use **external** information: use search engines; get **training**; get involved in **communities**; consult **experts** (see Monitoring, p49).

- Provide models or **scripts** for how to deal with common tickets.

- Have a way to **pass** a ticket to someone else – usually this means a Service Desk software tool. That someone might be a specialist in dealing with it (see Level 2 and 3 support, p35) or a boss because it is happening too slowly. The specialist might be in another organisation, which usually means email as the way of passing it to them, which has a risk of tickets getting lost, so have cross-checks and follow-up[2].

- Regularly **monitor** how long tickets are taking and chase up the slow ones.

You will also get value from tracking what **thing** was involved. If your service staff can associate interruptions and underlying problems and consumer requests with an asset, this soon gives you a picture of which things (and hence which makes and models) cause you the most grief.

Try applying a little **psychology** to interactions with consumers. These principles have proven to be effective[3]. Train your staff in them:

1) Get bad experiences over with early: talk about the difficult bits first.

2) Break up pleasure and combine pain: bring all the unpleasant bits together. Sprinkle the good news throughout the discussion.

3) Finish strongly: have a positive (scripted?) finish, emphasising the benefits to the consumer.

4) Give consumers choice: allow them to be in control as much as possible. Steer them but give them their rights.

5) Let consumers stick to their habits. Don't force change unless absolutely necessary. If the old way is good enough, leave it alone. When they must change, ease them across gradually.

---

[1] See Knowledge Centered Support (ref 9) for a method of improving how people store and use knowledge for support

[2] This is known as functional or horizontal escalation (between different groups dealing with it) and hierarchal or vertical escalation (sending it up the hierarchy of authority if it needs more senior attention)

[3] *Using behavioural science to improve the customer experience*, J DeVine, K Gilson, McKinsey Quarterly 2010 http://hbswk.hbs.edu/item/6201.html

Govern

Management runs the business; governance ensures that it is being run well and run in the right direction. It is the governor(s) who are **accountable**. In private enterprise, the governors are the owners or the owners' representatives, the Board. In the public sector they are the government. They should direct, monitor and evaluate all aspects of the business including service management[1]. They **direct** what the **strategy** (direction, objectives, goals) and **policy** (bounds, rules - often around finance, risk and compliance) should be. They don't direct how it is done – that's what managers are for.

Governors **monitor** through **notifications** and **reports** related to their directives, as frequently as they decide they need them. Ultimate accountability (legal and ethical) always comes back to the governors so they should verify reporting through independent audit.

They **evaluate** the feedback from **monitoring** to decide if the directives are going to be met, and whether they should change the directives based on what is going on inside and outside the organisation. They evaluate **plans** and **proposals**, and they make **decisions** on matters escalated to them.

Make sure your governors are governing; that everyone knows what the directives are; and that the governors get the information they need.

Before they can direct, monitor and evaluate, governors must perform one other essential action: **delegate**. In order to have governance, directors appoint an executive body to run the organisation, who in turn appoint managers to execute.

The service managers and staff need to provide "governance **enablement**": policy enforcement, strategy planning, measurement, audit, reporting. These activities aren't governance – they are the parts of operations that support and "plug into" governance: take direction, provide monitoring, propose ideas, escalate decisions. They often get referred to as governance but not in this book.

Governance enablement **cascades** down: you have policy specific to service management, and reporting specific to it. But the governance

---

[1] The international standard ISO/IEC 38500 describes the governance model of "direct-monitor-evaluate" which we use here. ISO/IEC 38500 is called "Corporate governance of information technology", but it is a governance model that can be applied anywhere.

itself always flows back to the organisation's governors. There is no such thing as service governance, only governance of service. The governors are responsible for service: the accountability cannot be delegated. Only the responsibility for management and governance-enablement can be delegated.

Governance directives, monitoring and evaluation should cover the following domains[1]:

- **Strategy**: communicating high-level goals and objectives; ensuring they are known and understood; and confirming that management plans of all kinds are in accordance.
- **Risk**: determining acceptable levels; communicating them; ensuring risks are owned; monitoring risk reports and escalations.
- **Delegation**: the transfer of responsibility and ownership down into the organisation; its acceptance and fulfilment by staff; and the flow of accountability back to the governors.
- **Performance**: selecting metrics, assessments and benchmarks for delivery of value; letting people know they are monitored; and ensuring useful and accurate data is reported back.
- **Compliance**: ensuring all requirements are identified and owned; assuring those requirements are being met; or understanding the risks where they are not.
- **Culture**: clearly setting expectations of behaviour and projecting the organisational culture; ensuring management and staff understand and adopt.
- **Capability**: ensure the organisation has the personnel, infrastructure and resources to perform current operations; to respond quickly enough to change; and to meet anticipated future demands.
- **Procurement**: setting policy; approving major relationships; ensuring transparency, appropriateness, fiscal sense and balance across portfolios.

Remember "People, Practices and Things"? We've covered People and Practices. Once you've started improving them, you can move on to Things: tools, artefacts, information, stuff...

---

[1] This is our own list. ISO38500 only lists six.

Tools, technology, forms, books and all other objects we use in delivering service are Things (Things is our word – don't go looking for it in any textbooks). Don't let staff **fixate** on Things. Managing and improving service is about people and culture, and practices and procedures, not Things. Things help people do practices better – they make good people more efficient and/or more effective at doing good practices. Better Things don't fix bad practice or bad culture.

Computing

Information technology (IT) is an essential part of most services. IT is always **complex** and inherently **unstable**. It needs rigorous **control** and **professionalism** to deliver it effectively and reliably.

IT can be managed as an **internal** service in its own right using the techniques in this book. Some of the most mature service and process management in your organisation should be in IT.

One way to obtain this maturity (and also efficiency) is by **outsourcing** IT services. This often comes at a cost in flexibility and innovation. You can outsource IT operations, but think hard before you outsource planning or governance-enablement of IT.

Service Desk

You will soon grow to need a service-desk **software tool** to track all the "registers" of things (see Respond). Find a tool general to business, not IT-specific. You can purchase software, or there are a number of tools available as "software as a service" (SaaS) on the internet.

Almost all of them are good enough. Make sure you can:
- define **workflow**: automate the passing of a ticket from one group to another depending on what it is about.
- **clone** one type of ticket from another: e.g. make a problem from an incident; a change from a request
- set **alerts** when things take too long
- search a **knowledgebase** based on what is in the ticket

Assets

As we already mentioned, you will also get value from tracking all your assets. You probably do this already as part of procurement/ purchasing/ fixed assets. There are usually good quick returns to be had by managing assets better: not **losing** them; knowing what is under **warranty** and by which provider; **depreciating** properly; tracking when **leases** expire; controlling the number of **instances** of licensed assets e.g. software, or patented technology.

See if there is value in making that asset data more **accessible** to the seven areas of service management, especially Provide and Respond. Once you do this, you will want to broaden your definition of "asset" to other Things that services depend on, such as paper-based systems, external systems, documents, and people.

Impact

Once you have asset data, the next step is to be able to deduce which services are **depending** on an asset so that you know the service **impact** of something happening to that asset, either something planned (Plan, Change) or unplanned (Incident).

Vendors offer tools to record these **relationships**, and even in some cases to work them out (**discover**) automatically. The alternative is to work it out manually **on-demand** each time. Look at the total costs and value of either approach.

Monitoring

In any business the ability to see the **status** of a service end-to-end across your supply chain seems desirable. It is not easy. Vendors will want to sell you solutions. Before you get into the complexity of trying to compose a comprehensive picture of service bit-by-bit from the bottom up, ask yourself whether you can test it more simply by monitoring the consumer **experience**. Monitor the service by putting dummy transactions in and seeing what comes back; or by monitoring real transactions. If transactions are IT-based you can buy tools to do it for you. If not, get your support staff to interact via phone or whatever channels exist to enter orders for service/product and requests for response. Monitor the result, e.g. retail businesses do this with "mystery shoppers".

It is almost always more accurate and cheaper to monitor the health of a service by treating it as a "black box" and measuring it from the outside, instead of trying to see and measure every single bit of the internals. The downside of the black box approach is that if things do go wrong, it doesn't give you the tools to **drill down** to see why.

To drill down you need more sophisticated monitoring of **underlying** systems and individual **components**. The top priority with systems monitoring is to consolidate monitoring into a single **console** into which all messages flow and from which all responses originate. Those responses might be humans seeing the message, or automated actions to deal with it or to raise an alert.

Information

Knowledge is what is inside people's heads. Dealing with that is beyond the scope of this book, but you do need to organise information to provide good service. Keep information somewhere[1] **safe**, **accessible** and **indexed.** This won't happen or it won't stay that way unless somebody has accountability for looking after it – a **librarian**.

Information includes
- a catalogue of services (see Provide, p34)
- documentation of each service solution (see Solve, p26)
- contracts and agreements
- manuals and other technical information
- practices, processes and work procedures
- assets
- consumers, customers, suppliers and partners
- help, training
- interactions, responses, problems and interruptions
- workarounds and resolutions to respond to consumer requests

Outside sources of information are as important as internal. The internet in general and Google in particular are the obvious example.

The lines between internal and external information are blurring. Websites out of your control will provide product information and support for your services. Your consumer **community** will communicate with each other and with you in public forums such as websites and Twitter. You cannot control this – only **participate**.

---

[1] This is called a knowledgebase though we prefer the term informationbase

As promised,

FIFTY PAGES!!

(If you are reading a digital version of this
book you just have to believe us)

We'd like to hear from you.

Did this book have **meaning** for you?   Did it address what you do and
what you need?

Did the book have **value** for you?   Did it give you a return?

Tell us your service management story at www.basicsm.com.   It helps us
serve you better, and with your consent we might feature your case study
on the website.

The author welcomes feedback – good or bad – as part of our own
continual service improvement.   Contact us at www.basicsm.com.

Please place reviews on Amazon to tell others what you thought of this
book.

Finally, look in to the www.basicsm.com website regularly to check for
updates, new resources, and possibly new editions of this book.

What next

Some parts of this book may be enough information for you to manage your services, for now and maybe forever. Almost certainly though, in other parts you will need to know and do more. As well as the references provided within this book, visit the website at www.basicsm.com for more sources, and for forums to discuss with others where to go from here. Here are some general bodies of knowledge around service management and especially service improvement that you may find useful for your next growth step.

Services in general

To learn more about service management, look at USMBOK and the Service Management 101 website (ref 1).

Also study the discipline of product management which has much in common with service management.

For further improvement of your service management, you could look to quality frameworks such as Six Sigma, Total Quality Management, or Baldrige.

You may want to certify your organisation, both for the external reference value to customers and for the internal growth required to step up to it. You can certify with:

- CMMI-SVC

- Baldrige

- ISO9003 for services, ISO9001 if manufacturing a product

For call centres, consider certifying to the COPC-2000® CSP Standard http://www.copc.com/standards.aspx

IT Services

If you are a small organisation, consider FITS www.becta.org/fits as your framework of practices.

If you are a larger or more complex organisation, then look at COBIT www.isaca.org/cobit as a framework. Flesh out COBIT with ITIL advice www.itil-officialsite.com.

Certify to eSCM, COBIT, ISO27001, or ISO20000-1.

Resources

This book uses ideas from the following sources.

Useful to any services organisation

Did we mention you should visit www.basicsm.com to see if there are any supplementary pages for your industry or other special interests? This book is just the right size that you can print on A4 or Letter, fold them and tuck them into the book. The website also has updates to the book, a forum for discussion, and other useful stuff including checklists, articles and links.

Frameworks

1. USMBOK, Universal Service Management Body of
    Knowledge™ www.usmbok.org
    *The Guide to the Universal Service Management Body of
    Knowledge*, Ian Clayton, Tahuti (2008), ISBN: 978-0981469102

USMBOK is a website and a book, a big book, "a definitive guide to service management". This is *the* guide, 450 pages describing everything you need to consider for service management end-to-end across the business – the gold-standard best practice. It occasionally reveals its IT roots. If you get serious about service management, buy it.

2. CMMI-SVC, http://www.sei.cmu.edu/cmmi/tools/svc/

Carnegie Mellon University developed the CMM models for measuring process maturity. Most of these models are IT-centric. One model, the CMMI-SVC, is not specific to IT. It is a generic model for providing services (though much of the internet talk about it is IT-oriented).

CMMI-SVC is an excellent body of knowledge, comprehensive and well structured. It is also free to download, and you can certify your organisation against it. On the other hand the language and structure is esoteric, quite impenetrable. Expect a tough read.

Changing people

3. *The 8-Step Process of Successful Change*, John Kotter,
    http://www.ouricebergismelting.com/html/8step.html is the

most widely accepted model for getting organisations to change.

Service management books

There are many books about "service". Some focus on across-the-counter services, and/or the culture of service more than the practice. Others take a more general view of services and consider service *management*, like this book, but often get very academic and comprehensive instead of looking for the pragmatic core. For the record, we like:

4. *Service Management and Operations*, **Haksever, Render, Russell and Murdick, Prentice Hall(2000), ISBN: 0-13-081338-9**

...which is still in print.

In addition, the study of product management overlaps service management a great deal (products and services being ends of the same continuum remember) so there are a bunch more books on that topic.

Look on www.basicsm.com for a bibliography.

IT-centric resources

Basic Service Management is drawn from a number of sources that are specific to IT and not necessarily useful to the general service management reader. Sources such as ITIL®...

5. **IT Infrastructure Library, www.itil-offialsite.com**

...are useful only if you are an Information Technology service provider, in which case they are pretty good (if expensive). For IT, the five core ITIL books are the generally accepted "standard" approach to service management.

For other readers ITIL may be too IT-centric, with the possible exception of the first of the five main books in ITIL...

6. *ITIL Service Strategy*, **OGC, TSO (2007), 978-0113310456**

...which is a dense, heavy book describing business strategy for the provision of IT services. [As this book was being prepared, *Service Strategy* was undergoing a rewrite to make it more accessible, expected in late 2011].

If you think you can get value from an IT book, instead of ITIL we would recommend...

7. *IT Service Management An Introduction*, **Jan van Bon, Van Haren (2007) ISBN: 978-90-8753-051-8**

...and any publications related to COBIT from...

8. **www.isaca.org**

...and KCS for organising your people, processes and tools to make better use of knowledge for the support of services or products

9. *Knowledge Centered Support*,
   www.serviceinnovation.org/knowledge_centered_support

Outsourcers of IT service and those using them should refer to ...

10. *eSCM*, **http://itsqc.cmu.edu**

There are a few original ideas of the author's in this book too, first published on the websites *Core Practice* (www.corepractice.org), *He Tangata* (www.hetangata.com) and *The IT Skeptic* (www.itskeptic.org).

About the author:

Rob England is a service management consultant and commentator. He has twenty years experience mapping business requirements to IT solutions, ten of them in service management. He is active in the itSMF (the professional body for ITSM). He is the author of a popular blog www.itskeptic.org, a humorous book *Introduction to Real ITSM*, four other IT books, and a large number of articles, papers and presentations – see www.twohills.co.nz.

He lives with his wife and son in a small house in a small village in a small country far away.

internal service provider - what is our service?

~~what do they need / value (analyze).~~
~~What is our product?~~
~~What are the customers problems~~

1. what is our product?
2. where do we market?
3. what are the customers problems?
4. what do they need / value?
5. How do we communicate to them?
6. what is our value?

Made in the USA
Columbia, SC
13 September 2019